over
under
fed

over under fed

Amy Marguerite

First published 2025
Auckland University Press
Waipapa Taumata Rau
University of Auckland
Private Bag 92019
Auckland 1142
New Zealand
www.aucklanduniversitypress.co.nz

ISBN 978 177671 164 2

Published with the assistance of Creative New Zealand

A catalogue record for this book is available from the National Library of New Zealand.

Design by Duncan Munro

This book was printed on FSC® certified paper

Printed in Singapore by Markono Print Media Pte Ltd

For the quietly immoderate

I am still waiting for the right words to explain myself to you.
When there was nothing left to smoke, I drew on my lips with a pen until they were black.

— Allison Benis White, *Please Bury Me in This*

Contents

terms and conditions

far too blue

i have grown appendages of contempt
for many things. i believe in god because people
are too digestible. i am terrible at staying
in touch unless you are exceptionally interesting
which means you either chew grass or chew gum
like grace paley. i inherited my cheekbones from no one.
i feel abandonment like a baby left alone for half
a minute but can't cry about it because fluoxetine
exchanged that privilege for PURE ELATION.
i give up at once on anything i cannot immediately be
brilliant at. *i would rather feast on a decaying twig*
doused in petrol than play chess with your children, claudia.
my parents never put the correct number of candles
on my cakes. i am tired of pretending i don't want
to be greedy. i have conditioned my body to house-sit
dead ends for pleasure. i dream of the day my eyes
are the seeds of a green bell pepper. the world is already
far too blue and squinting   at what light.

reuptake inhibitor

this sunday is full
to the brim
with sadness.

everything that should be lovely
clouds
my little sister's smile

presses deep
on a pressure point
and keeps pressing until

an electric feeling
arrives at the base
of my skull.

from here.
the lovely thing
(that i do not know

to be lovely yet)
ascends to the pleasure
centre of the brain

quick enough
to be realised
but not experienced

(equal in magnitude
to an unrequited love)
and for a small moment

i think i get it
why people choose
loveliness over sorrow.

an actual tear
falls. but
i do not get to choose.

every sunday
is a prayer i cannot
send up because

i am too aware
of the comedown. it seems
a cliff is only dangerous

after you jump off
of it and i am so tired
of jumping.

somehow or other
my body is returned
by the same ocean

the one that keeps
forgetting to part
in the middle

always
projectile vomiting
itself onto the same sand

in one big
unrefined heap.
this

is where i dwell
among the currents bound
to a predictable path.

at the end
of the day
i just want to be lovely.

trust at 33,000 feet

this sky is sangria dregs
in a chipped luminarc mug
a clingstone nectarine
in a paper bag in the boot
of your ex-lover's
dynamic blue mazda demio
a hot artery on dry ice
gasoline the moment it realises
it is gasoline.

this is what it is to be
voluntarily combustible
exactly what you expected.

those who open sky
before land
open the world expecting
something else.
your prayers
have always tasted so much
like watered-down pleas
you've never needed to actually
believe them.

place your feet and knees together
with your feet firmly on the floor.
tuck chin into chest.
do not tamper with the emergency exit.

had you braced for impact
this sky might've let you down.

pesky limbic system

i took two extra tart cherry capsules to relax myself last night
because i was fighting and flighting too much over the woman
who put herself inside me last week. my therapist tells me love
is supposed to be a remedy. my grandmother tells me love
is supposed to live in a body. love only occasionally enters me
and when it does i am no emptier than a full stop at the end
of a self-help book. emptiness is still loveliness. loveliness
is still the wrong word.

mount street cemetery

each time i contemplate
loving her
another cigarette is lit
in the wind.

am i supposed to be
laughing
because it's happening
so hard right now

like all the sparrows
are suddenly having
affairs in my mouth. they are
so caught up

in the optimism
of my plaque
they can't wonder why
hell is no longer

the clearing. but i am
just a corridor
for the reunion
of joints and why

shouldn't i be
proud of my ability
to tunnel?
my mother broke

a tooth on a shitty
liquorice strap.
she was watching tv
so it didn't really matter.

july poem

should i just
get chummy with this
unwhole thing
it's a familiar
breed of terrible
and i can do that
i can touch
the housefly
so many
times hate it
and keep it happening.
i've always been
weird about
contentment
contentment
the word itself
is claustrophobic
who stuffed so
many ts in there
and how come
tittering is so
cavernous. it's not
a problem that
i want to sit
at the hem
of everything
watch the dog
fall asleep
with her eyes
sort of open
i'm never the centre
of a dream
nobody's told me that
i just know
like i know
there is such a thing
as a stupid question.
there's this one
particular skirt

every middle-aged
woman wears
and it is actually so
ugly. i could spread
it on my toast
each morning
and weep.
it's like if linkedin
were a type of
fabric and what makes me
want to kiss that. today
is the shortest
day and it's dragging.
the ulcers
in my mouth
are healing and
that's called relief
but what is it
actually called.
i'm not angry
at the ulcers for being
there i'm angry
at my body for taking
so long to heal
i can't hate the pain
anymore
that's work
like questioning
the dream
in the dream
or convincing
someone to walk
in the rain without
a raincoat.
i'm shocked
that most cars
don't have cd players
in them now.
zita says i'm late
to the party

but i've just been
mixing this tape
in another room
peeking through
the same bridges
like some
unstuffed swan
and where do i put
the minutes
that don't fit?
i feel like a hairdresser
turning away
the kids with headlice
and that's not fair
but that's exactly
what it is.
i told my father
i didn't get the residency
and he said oh well
go to denmark
instead and i might
just do that
drag my body through
a whole thought
i didn't have
wouldn't that be
the dream?

discharge notes (i)

i was at the kebab shop with my sister
when jean and her husband said hello
but actually the husband said nothing.
i know jean because she was on the same ward
as my mother when my mother was sick
pregnant with me. they had a competition going
whose kid will come out first. jean won
by i think three days theo did that but jean
got the flowers. i wanted to marry theo
in primary school grace beat me to it
had the wedding on a wet-weather day
in room thirty-two. i was so sad depressed
about it even we were obviously soulmates
our mothers knew each other before
we were born. anyway i hadn't seen jean
in such a long time. she said she had been
thinking about me that week which was
a beautiful sort of strange and she didn't
have to explain her thinking beyond that
but she did. whenever a person does that i listen
because it's probably important.
i'm always hoping it's a dream i was in
i fucking love being in people's dreams.
jean said she had recently started working
at saint katherine's hospital had spoken to lisa
and thought of me. lisa was and clearly still is
one of the eating disorder specialists there
quite nuts because i had also been
thinking about lisa that week and julie
but mostly lisa. i was thinking i should
thank them for everything they did for me
like tell my parents to stop supplying
liquorice tea but when jean asked if i was
doing well i didn't say yes i am because of that
but i actually did. i don't think a body ever
forgets lovely women.

love language

limerence

why do i obsess over people
who understand me?
i ask google
i ask the old testament
i ask the sibilant wail behind
my wisdom tooth.
i can feel the disappointment
in my ex-therapist's voice
like lukewarm beer
down my merino
there is never only one answer
to a question like that.
but i need *one.*
my dreams are becoming
too particular.
my poetry is firing
steel-capped neurons
at the waistline of
stale grief. my grandmother is
crying over her life
in the conservatory and i
have forgotten how to
partition my love. i put it all in
an envelope on the
fifth of february
and sent it to auckland.
now it is holy saturday.
i'm still not sure
if my love was delivered.

*

the catholic church
down the road
is commemorating
the harrowing of hell.
i wonder if jesus dreamt
of this day between
rock and linen.
i wonder if they are still dreaming
taking three days

to get out of bed
in the morning
four more to get back
to sleep again.
i'm beginning to believe god
invented homeostasis
just to have a go
at fucking something up
and after a few goes
saw that insomniacs
had a high probability
of acquiring the gift of discernment.

insomniacs also
have a high probability
of fantasising
about threesomes
with their teacher
and the woman who divulged
her recent heartbreak
over beer pong
but we keep this from god
so we can keep doing it.

*

perhaps the good things
that come to those who wait
are the leftovers
of those who have
already waited.
perhaps they are still waiting
recording the seconds between
seen and delivered
on the underside
of a used napkin
wondering if
it could be more productive
to live through
an insoluble wound
than around a solid solution.

the flame, it takes

nobody considers
the flame it takes
to lose a head
the catatonic drum
of wax betraying
one side of the brain then the other.

i maintain a peculiar
fondness
for that
interior dampness
that *sway*
of matter like a seesaw
or seagull fleeing
beckoning
messing with resistance.

when it happens i think
of you
your shellac eyeballs
smouldering into mine
how after some time it becomes......   and we both look away
in a hurry
to the floor or
highly strung painting
on the wall.

we both just let it
drip
sway
set us completely (coolly)
ablaze.

stalling

all night i had you.
i went to press
a warm thumb
against your eyelid this morning
but when i rolled over
my greyhound huffed
a grand huff at my jawbone
............bitch
breath dandelioning
my dreaming
i keep thinking
about apologising
for not holding your left hand
when my right one
was stupidly clammy
with unavoidable
logic. but my hand
was probably joking.
my limbs suspend disbelief
more readily than
an immortal jellyfish
drafting its seventeenth will.
i'd carve out spare time
to put you in one
of my wills because
it's queer as fuck
to compliment your slayer
but quasi-regretfully
i'll have you know
(before anything
gets *too unserious*)
that i don't have
spare time for spare time.
i'm too busy wondering what now
we would be in
if i had let my wine-
dry lips scutter
crabwise down your cheek.
but wondering is
brutally futile and

an apology is
the equivalent of a kiss
and i WOULD
much rather KISS YOU
if i couldn't see myself
apologising for it later.
anyway
the bullock track is
a jealous gradient
no place for a moment really.
but i wouldn't have minded
pissing off a few
uber drivers if it had meant
stalling our
situation/ship......?
into some sort of
phantasmagoric
lesbian devotion......?......??
i mean
i keep getting emails
saying my dropbox
is full and i don't know how
to add more storage
i mean *us*
is taking a fucking
manatee gestation
period to download
and......well......
i'm deleting my cat pics
for you.

love language

a metre apart
in that photo
i don't want
to have to convince
everyone
we're closer in that
gorgeous other way
i listen to
a song about
whiskey and
throwing up
think that's
a fucking sick
devotion and skip lunch.
i might kiss
nobody
at the party tonight
a strategy i devised
still drunk in
your shower
one morning
ages ago
fingered another
name on
the window
a little gift
for you really
i am so off
the market
i've put a cap on
the amount
of eileen myles
i'm allowed
to consume
in a day and
that's saying
about as much
as rebecca
with the blue
tick. i want to

gift you her
painting of a
jersey stuck
halfway between
someone's head
and wherever
they are going
to put it next.

don't you want to know
you are adored
rebecca

don't you
want to waste
your entire lunch
break wondering
how?

without any kissing
at all.

shadowboxing a situationship

aching after
all that 6-3-2
1-1-6 could've
outed your
phone number
hard gone
viral with
my aching
for a reason
haven't
memorised it
won't can't
be bothered
2 slabs
of lasagne
for 2 strong
arms useless
dream of an-
other woman no
sex just saving
her from
something
you said
talk soon
that was 5
days ago almost
25 now and may is
full of birth-
days not mine
my sister's and
mother's
i remember
being my mother's
age *see*
you soon
that was 5
years ago
pinkie ache
blame the glove
teaspoon

in a dishwasher
remember
wide air fish-
hook proof
of anything
at least 1
person really
wanted
seal the
piñata and there's love
in that and i
have some
weird faith in that
juvenile
arousal
flame before
the bones
grow up *bird*
crap wind-
shield wipe
a phoney ventricle
fuck active
recovery
what actual
fool promises
to jog on
the spot
i wanna leap year
round the clock
roundhouse kick
my want
candelabra
through this
ache and what app isn't
a second peek
at god?

discharge notes (ii)

a few years ago i decided i'd write
a list of all the women i owe my life to
even the women who have hurt me
a lot like claudia. it was overwhelming
not to write to carry so i deleted the
phone note wrote a letter to claudia
instead. gratefulness is sore you can't
ever expect anyone to feel how they made you
feel especially if they've never almost
been dead. jean didn't recognise my sister
at the shop said you must have gone
to school with amy but she looks so much
like me even i see it now the way i
still have a problem with things that just
keep mattering like buying normal coke.

jean's gone home now anorexia went
when i buried the tube in the ground
doing well and gemma died that day.

infidelity

i arrive at the berth
with your children.
the shallows whisper
sleep song into engine ear.
the boy shows me
how to anchor but
i am too tired
to climb down the bow.
this water is so limpid
i am falling in
to a lucid dream
just by imagining it.
we lug our soggy bodies
onto public land.
the children swing
on broken swings.
the broken grown-ups
drink their drinks.
your husband crinkles
into the tarp
that single vessel
on his head pulsing
like the tiny clock
of an infant's heart.
i imagine the rupture
the division of
mind and matter
how painful it would be if
he actually ran for you.
when you arrive
late with the baggage
my feet make a triangle
shape around a starfish.
the girl etches angel
figures in the sand.
the grown-ups bury
their brokenness in
the overgrowth. you
pocket me in the thick of it
somewhere deep

somewhere damp
somewhere quietly
excessive. i can only
begin to imagine
the rapture of this
distance
        conditional
on a vision of what?
                        exactly.

or did i write that

you want to be
the kind of finger dipping
people do on a sunday
on monday i want to burn
all my diaries
in a roasting dish
full of carcass and root
somethings that didn't mean to come out
of the ground
they came out anyway
in a pair of gloves
familiar with the upside
imagine being born
with gloves
beneath your epidermis
the only thing outing you
the thought of them
there the other night
on the couch i told you
(i loved you)
my grandmother was raised
the wrong way around
(or did i write that in my diary)
on monday
i told you to put your fingers
in the dish
like a ceremony babe
like an organ recipient
gaining consciousness
as if the only matter
butchering *us*
is you

a disappointing piñata

everything she is
i am not
the world
has twelve
hundred fingers
none of them
are green none
have ever
touched me
except
in the wrong way
there are layers and
layers of lint
beneath my nails
my father
is paranoid
about the dryer
exploding sometimes i
light up inside
when the wind
makes my leg
hairs tremor
like unlicked
candyfloss
in bed my lover
wants to scissor
through the gale
force she needs
wrapping paper
to unmend
i don't
know how
to tell her i
am not that sort of
celebration

drives and drops

we were hitting the shuttlecock
and it started to rain and you
started singing and all of a sudden
i knew what i had to do to be good
at this game and the girl sat
beside the net complaining about
her body and the tide came
closer and sleep seemed further
away and the book i was supposed
to have finished was still on the couch
and i love the way you put your arm
around me there and i want you
to do it again and we are so wet now
it is time to get undressed and the
clothes stay on and the girl puts on
an accent and the net falls onto
the grass and this is so convincing
i might never read again and the boy
brings us beer and badminton is easier
when you're drunk and i am getting
so good at this and i am never
good at anything and everything
smells like the dinner we forgot
to take out of the oven and the ocean
that is so close i am already
swimming and let's just drop our
racquets

managing isolation

today we spoke
through glass.
i couldn't say
who was in the fish tank
you
or me?
or was the tank
an unmappable ocean
seducing us
from the outside in
and revealing
a new depth for our bodies
to inhabit?
it is impossible to tell
just by looking
at a jellyfish
how it is feeling
whether it is weeping
or smiling
or getting ready
to sting.
this encounter was
not so different.
you were not so
transparent as the
glass letting me
see you
and i would really like to
fold my leaden limbs
around your thin
frame again.
i would love to
hold you
and not worry
for the first time.
i really need you
to know that
these fourteen days
will draw more blood
than any rumour.

i picture myself
under covers.
i picture my cells
contracting.
i picture us splitting
the holy water
wringing until
it is useless.
i picture the days
thawing like morning
mist on a window
quickly
to begin
then slowly
more *effortfully*
as they're being watched.

gosh. your face

the steam
of your absence
lets me finger
print confessions
under the suboptimal
pressure of my
aro valley
showerhead

you kissed me
once
under water
lovelier than this
then told me
you couldn't go
any further

i felt the fear
on your back
in the cab that night
you were trembling
so honestly
i couldn't finish
the alphabet

O
fuck-me-when-you-can't-
make-out-my-lip-line
lover
there was nothing
super hideous
about the light

you didn't loathe it
once
on waiheke

you let me fondle
your thigh with my
doc marten
while the waiter
took our order

i remember thinking
gosh. your face
across the table
is the only view
my eyes
were born for

i would've held
you there forever
if the world
didn't need you
more

than anything

i wish
it was your voice
at the top
of the staircase

you could be
angrier at me
than the father
of your children

i would still
drop my towel and come
running

discharge notes (iii)

last night i was thinking about types
of vanishing my grandmother's
dentures in a chip packet someone's
favourite side of the bed making
their window littler than it definitely is.
when diaries get gritty you put them
in a shoe box call them gone. call them
one less segment of yourself to mourn
something like that. i keep so many secrets
from myself. like how i am really.
how i really felt about meghan trainor
at mealtimes having no beauty
to hold me at night i don't know maybe
my mother's god has MS uses a wheelchair
too maybe she has no idea how divine
that makes her seem and somewhere
there's a chicken kebab making someone
genuinely good for a moment the only
allowed transcendence. it's kinda like
we're meant to be usually crook.

every now and then my sister looks
at me a certain way the sort of stare
that could be mistaken for a well-meaning
bitch like if menstruation had a visage
i saw it in the parking lot in the song
i stopped singing to a tree at its funeral
but only because there wasn't one such a lack
of it with jean. it's not even that i was
buying myself a proper kebab going to
chew it well just how i didn't regurgitate
words. it's always terrified me that other people
can see you not the ones who do it
immediately i fucking love them like dreams
i mean the ones who hoard clippings pin
them to the right hemisphere because
they foolishly give a shit. my sister wants me
to want to be seen by her and i suppose
i need to want that too. but all the hankerings
i've ever had have nothing to do with need.
the body my wellness lets people unsee.

ward 25a

when my body was *Amorphophallus titanum*

i couldn't stay still long enough to read a haiku.
i didn't kiss my boyfriend back in the cinema or ever.
i wore thermals to the beach in december.
my doctor told me to *just drink more blue-top milk.*
my father no longer wanted to hug me.
my teachers were uncomfortably friendly.
my little sister spied on me with a fake instagram account.
my skin turned orange from eating too many carrots.
i thought i was vegan for environmental reasons.
i had the bone density of someone six years my junior.
i dropped the same university paper three times.
i made friends i wouldn't be allowed to keep.
i hoarded medical supplies envelopes anything disposable.
i walked through fire tunnels to be healed.
i walked through fire tunnels to be held.
believers gathered round the experimental subject
intubated her
bathed her
put a watch at her bedside.
                                        she ran to the wintergardens when she realised
she was dying.

fortisip

there was never enough caramel in stock
everyone wanted the caramel
banana reminded me of the perky nana my mother gave me
when i fell off my scooter and grazed my shin   i cried so much
they replaced it with strawberry
strawberry reminded me of the mcdonald's milkshake
i chucked out the car window
on my way to the hospital   i cried so much
they replaced it with a tube
                                        i cried
                                                        out of my nose

raisins

six years ago i decided
i fucking hated men.

shortly after that
i decided i fucking
hated fucking men
so i kept fucking them.

one of the men
i fucked told me i
had a beautiful figure.

i had only eaten a few
raisins that day so i kept eating
only raisins so i could keep being
beautiful for the fucking men
i kept hating and fucking.

discharge notes (iv)

whenever i think about the friends
i wasn't allowed to keep i think i hate
lisa and julie for ruining my life. i don't
know if they are alive now i hope they are
doing gorgeous things like anything.
friends in hospital are like friends
at school you don't have to have them
but it does make a whole lot of sense
the whole experience a lot more laughable
if you do like the time ashley taught me
how to get away with water loading
before my five a.m. weigh-in ha ha.
i was really good at being sick it felt good.
to be good at something. bad to be good
at something bad so weird how so many
people don't have an expiration instinct
at the very least a morbid curiosity
to get them through the day! but a web is not
a safety net in the real world nobody
tells you that prepares you for the new
collapse. basted with gaunt drippings.

drip irrigation

(i)

all our elsewheres are also here
in the emergency unit.

we don't enjoy eating so they feed us
through umbilical cords.

we tell them we are plants
we can produce our own food.

(ii)

nobody listens here
in the emergency unit but babies

hear everything. the girl
in the bed beside me

is cutting her cord with a pair of teeth
she found in her mouth.

thick beige fluid trickles down
her chin before coating her

sheets like a lullaby.
not everyone gets the chance

to be soothed. some of us
die trying.

(iii)

an old man tells his wife he
can't wait to be elsewhere.

the girl in the bed beside me
has drifted off in a pond of goo

little green shoots forming
a ring around her.

afterthought

you won't believe me but
i was never empty
your drip feed never fed me
i alone had plenty to feast on

eyes
so many
eyes

could've saved
everyone
a lot of money
and blood noses

quasi recovery

bee
you remind me of the one
i took out of my pool
the way you hug your little legs
around the stem of that leaf
as i look away
thinking you will be ok
on your own.

bee
some things need saving
more than once.

i was hungry

o pancreatic weather
recreational creature
where is your beatitude?

i prescribe a theatrical treatment
wheat pack and breathable
leather sweatshirt.

caveats are just eggbeaters
for the meatless.
you do not feature in that wreathy repeatability!

o heathenry pinfeather
uncreated creature
just eat.

discharge notes (v)

there are a bunch of abbreviations
i just can't get behind like when i was in
creative writing class and everyone
referred to their MS the way it was nearly
finished or in the fucking bin. i want to
put my mother's in the fucking bin.
i don't know if i can ever get pregnant
it might matter that's the thing you don't
think about the later there wasn't one
window littler than it definitely was
just tubes to think through hurt a mother.
when i was discharged the third time
my father read the notes in front of me.
ED for ED. admitted to both they didn't
record the latter it comes with years
mothers they're too proud to thank i get it
i do. rozi plain has this song it came on
in the car on the way to work yesterday
called 'prove your good' i was driving so
i couldn't check was it your or you're
had to listen hard remember jean   it's neither.

hollowing full

only womb

let yourself submerge
in a puddle
of your own remaking.

permission sees
the unseeable shift from
nothingness
to nothingness with
a ripple of renaissance.

resistance strangles
even those attempts spurred by
pure conviction.

don't let yourself
half-arse it.

don't be fooled by anyone
who says this
is an end, either.
a pool of water is the only womb
we choose to enter.

i once wrote in a poem
a cliff is only dangerous
after you jump off
of it.

that was before
i realised i am terrified
of heights.

a puddle is only dangerous
before you submerge in it
and by submerge
i mean suspend
and by suspend
i mean surrender
and by surrender
i mean stop
looking up for an answer.

measuring (in)sincerity

if every prayer is a plea
why am i still waiting to be
realised? i have mastered
the ritual. i should be seriously
remarkable by now. but all my gods
are goal posts   ghosts
good health cannot move
through. i am the reason ironing
boards have covers
as useless as the hail
mary after skipping a meal.
i am a miracle   offcut.
i am a doctrine-hooded   heretic.
a whole bunch of us
were expecting a difference
between sent up and
given up by now.
        what is disappointment

if not

        a huge   relief.

forecasting hindsight

a swarm of wasps took your veil
and hissed it down the overbridge
under which you were once
a temporary thing spinning your
guileless gossamer and spitting your
lies vermillion like an *accidental*
cayenne pepper paprika situation

you were so committed then
to prising other anatomies apart
savouring their surrender as though
they were actually giving themselves up
as if you weren't just undressing
a nostalgic aroma so as to feel a little bit
new

you (quite simple human) have stolen too much

i composed a beautiful
sleepless nightmare and it
has all gone. a quite simple human
(you)
perhaps wouldn't even feel it.
a little gap.
a ph ase that would lose its reality.
whereas with me it is even more than i
could have believed
a squeal of pain essential.
i suppose people say
these things spoil love
like this - but oh my dear

you have no idea how i
love. but you
resent it.

i bore you with

the shaky. i shall have
to

stop at here we are
and
buy a stamp. even this will have to go.

[THE WATERFALLS WERE
SO LOVELY
ALL BLANKETED IN SNOW.]

we're going to have to wait.

sometimes joy

little joy, hello!
i feel brushstrokes, like tendrils,
sweep my scrapbook flesh!

so

this is my joyride to the new inferno so
i give my body to a complex intersection so
my features can be urban and implausibly linear so
i will blossom like a streetlamp in july so
there is a reason i don't leave so
i am an exclamation mark in disarray so
you can use me as a coat hanger so
i am a limited edition trelise cooper frill of a lifetime dress so
why the fuck do you only take me out on rainy days so
the shape of me will melt like cold-pressed oil into you so
i am the impression/ideal so
you are the artist/realist so
i will eventually be the chosen one so
fucking original so
all kinds of weather so
ridiculously stripped of your umbra

over under fed

i am trying a new thing
where i don't rely on toxin to grow pupils.

this might be
the way i am now

bulging lucid barrels
overflowing with offerings

sprightly with the season that has me
shedding leaves

and finding them again
settled above a disturbed layer.

this could be
how i am now

suddenly everywhere
everything suddenly

the meat i left with the midwife
a holy sanguine tossing roars at a wall

some sweat
some rib

a corporeal cauldron welding
a contemporary sort of mammal

so rabidly sober it might leak
its insides out

dilate and combust
very delicately.

this is
why i am then

perceiving these limbs
studying them

slowly.
kindly.

a little bit
casually.

these are the forgotten stems
of twenty-five springs

the tentacles
of a dilapidated angel

combing her sorrow
with some long-lost strength

preparing her ringlets
for the new disease.

predisposed

i also backstroked to avoid ingesting mother's woe ~~was real real was woe woe was my mother's orry sorry mother i also.~~

home to you

cate le bon wrote a song called
what i called this poem it's
4.13 i want a beer and paul's
celebrating his graduation
at the bar i'm invited and that's
so nice. it's usually a bad sign
when i just want to drink
alone. it wasn't usually bad
until claudia i got so ill then
better again when she went
to england and stayed there.

a week before i moved to melbourne
i told helen that i had fallen
in love. she said *that's usually*
what happens and i nodded
at the screen like it had
happened before. it's maybe
like finally writing the poem
for the first time like finally
telling that difference to matter.

tonight i'll put on james salter's
reading of 'break it down'
wait as i usually do for the old shirt.
i don't dread the endings of
things i'm going to have to
leave that somehow unlearn
autumn and get a job. but
my desire is not entirely over
in this place i'm still unleashing
pathetic furniture stopgaps for
when the beer fails and it does that
a lot up half the night without you.

i think so many stories are
flights we forget to run for
bridges we can't drape across
the feeling only ever properly
borrowed if i never give
it back. i'm sick of the torch on

everything. that's always
not mine. hung up on all that
true pretending like an unrequited
apparition old shirt without
ever actually calling it old and
there's the usual design. i'm
not incapable of it just unfit
to adequately adore it compromise
the corporeal sconce how it
makes me real. are you as well
drinking alone with ungood thoughts.
reimagining that home to.
that home
too.

keep this true

for blair

i jokingly suggest you change
your relationship status to
it's complicated and i'll change
mine to *engaged* we have exactly
six mutual friends on here probably
a matt and you know which freckles
to kiss to keep this true call them
fret markers or like don't when
bree asks if we're......official
is that the rehearsal what steve albini
wrote in his letter to nirvana
the licking pattern of which dog
at the bowl it's only complicated
if you paraphrase the dream
in which i meet you at the airport
with my girlfriend because i love you
like no amen at all and meaningful clutter
is a brilliant title for a poem
or a song......i won't call this that you can
have it i'm not even talking about
your house just maybe a busy gap
our bodies on a sunday the novel somebody
else writes on the plane in this
heat anything is nowhere else a thing
i used to have a thing for and
this is new and great and new and pinched
harmonics in my search bar

discharge notes (vi)

to the nurse who called the hospital
my second home actually fuck you.
a home is harsh even when *it is* yours
your home was harsh because you
said it was mine *mi casa es su casa*
claudia fuck you too. i wonder if
a tree ever feels itself empty in autumn
the same way an autumn feels itself empty
of home an affair that doesn't halt
at confession a small child smiling and
what is it about money making everything
possible like breakfast and depression
nothing like a degree to disappear a father's disgust.
i'm genuinely curious. where do people *think*
recovery happens. when the desire to be
different is true there's a kitchen in that
call it maybe a good bedroom my best friend
died in one of those i miss her every day.

i used to record myself eating on my webcam
thought it was interesting might help
a person in the future save them even
and i wasn't only eating i was talking too
about lovely women before i knew
who they were. the whole time i was just
trying to be better was just thinking
that somewhere in the rind of it all it wasn't
just mine never would be nearly finished.

put it in a list in a diary a mouth
a tube in the ground something like that
a kebab a husband a sister her stare even i
see it now. the way she had a problem
with things that forgot to start mattering
like her looking so much. like me.

margaret

susan

lauren

maree

gemma

ashley

lisa

julie

anna-rose

zita

alana

kata

jenny

anna

helen

virginia

florence

eileen

claudia

Notes and Acknowledgements

The epigraph quotes *Please Bury Me in This* by Allison Benis White (Four Way Books, 2017).

'far too blue' alludes to Grace Paley's exceptionally amusing habit of chewing gum during readings.

'you (quite simple human) have stolen too much' uses as source material a letter from Vita Sackville-West to Virginia Woolf, 21 Jan 1926, found at *Letters of Note*, https://news.lettersofnote.com/p/i-just-miss-you-in-a-quite-simple/

'so' is inspired by *Rue de Paris, temps de pluie (Paris Street; Rainy Day)*, 1877, a painting by Gustave Caillebotte.

'home to you' refers to James Salter's reading of 'Break it Down' by Lydia Davis, *Guardian* podcast, 23 May 2013, https://www.theguardian.com/books/audio/2013/may/23/james-salter-lydia-davis-break-it-down

Thank you to the editors of the following publications for giving some of these poems their first home: *Milly Magazine, Sweet Mammalian, Symposia Magazine, Starling, Turbine | Kapohau, bad apple,* Āporo Press's *Spoiled Fruit: Queer Poetry from Aotearoa*, The New Zealand Poetry Society's 2023 anthology *white-hot heart* and Paula Green's Poetry Shelf.

Thank you to Sam Elworthy and the wonderful team at Auckland University Press for so kindly and beautifully actualising this collection. Thank you to my lovely editor, Emma Neale, for engaging with these poems in such a way that prioritised tenderness and curiosity.

Thank you to the International Institute of Modern Letters, to my supervisor, Chris Price, and the MA class of 2022 for believing in my – positively chaotic – vision and providing a truly wild amount of support as I worked on (cried over) the first version of *over under fed*. Thank you to my undergraduate English Literature lecturers at Te Herenga Waka Victoria University of Wellington for their unfaltering warmth and enthusiasm. Thank you to Anna Jackson for her thoughtfulness and encouragement, and for making sure I didn't bin these poems!

Thank you to my grandmother for the recitations on the mezzanine floor and to my parents for their daily demonstrations of resilience. Thank you to my sister and best friend, Lauren, for being close through it all. Thank you to my darling partner, Blair, for his unconditional love and support, for locating pockets of silliness when I am blue and self-doubting, and for making the past year one of the most joyful years of my life. Thank you to my dearest friends: Anna-Rose, Zita, Alana, Kata, Jenny, Eden, Mina, Lex, Kieran, Anna, Helen, Marianne.

Thank you to Virginia Woolf and Eileen Myles, my literary lifelines.

Thank you to Maree for promising loveliness after anorexia – she was so right.

Amy Marguerite is a poet and essayist based in Tāmaki Makaurau. In 2022, she completed an MA in Creative Writing with distinction at the International Institute of Modern Letters. Her poetry has appeared in anthologies including *Spoiled Fruit* and *white-hot heart* and has featured in literary journals, magazines and publications including *Starling*, *Turbine* and *Sweet Mammalian*. Her essay on the new generation of Aotearoa poets appears in Auckland University Press's forthcoming anthology *Te Whāriki*.